I'll Be There

(But I'll Be Wearing Sweatpants)

WORKBOOK

Finding Unfiltered, Real-Life Friendships in This Crazy, Chaotic World

Thirteen Lessons for Individuals and Groups

Amy Weatherly & Jess Johnston

I'll Be There (But I'll Be Wearing Sweatpants) Workbook

Requests for information should be addressed to:
HarperChristian Resources, 3900 Sparks Dr. SE, Grand Rapids, Michigan 49546

ISBN 978-0-310-15777-9 (softcover)

ISBN 978-0-310-15778-6 (ebook)

HarperChristian Resources titles may be purchased in bulk for church, business, fundraising, or ministry use. For information, please e-mail ResourceSpecialist@ChurchSource.com.

The authors are represented by Lisa Jackson / Alive Literary Agency.

First Printing March 2022 / Printed in the United States of America

Contents

Introduction

Hey, Can We Talk for a Sec?

At the core of our book, *I'll Be There (But I'll Be Wearing Sweatpants): Finding Unfiltered, Real-Life Friendships in This Crazy, Chaotic World,* was a heartfelt invitation, one that we put right in the book's introduction. Did you catch it there? The invite went like this: "Let's not do life alone; let's do it together."

Together.

There's so much hope in that word. So much promise and potential. Even if you're a die-hard introvert. Even if you're a self-starter, a solitude lover, an independence junkie. We're betting that you—yes, *even you*—see the value in having someone at your side from time to time, someone who sees you and gets you and loves you just like you are, someone who will lend an ear, or an egg, or a ride, or some hard-won wisdom when the bottom falls out of life. In fact, our bet is that every woman reading these words not only sees the value in relational connectivity but actually *craves that connectivity for herself.* If she could just sort out how to overcome the (totally valid) obstacles that keep her living life alone, she would overcome them in a heartbeat.

She would show up.

She would invest in others' lives.

She would let herself be known.

She would *friend*. She would friend *hard*.

If you fall into that category of wanting the "together" dream but having no clue how to bring it to fruition, then you're in the right place. We've both been there. We still visit there every once in a while. But we no longer live there 24/7. We've landed a new address, and to shoot straight with you, the view is much better from here. It can be much better for you, too.

So, while we're by no means experts in this friending thing, we're not as hopeless as we once were. And maybe since we still remember the sinking wretchedness of feeling all alone in this world, we're just the right people to lead you to higher ground.

* * *

In the thirteen lessons that follow, you'll be offered a boatload of opportunities to assess your friendship landscape as it stands today, as well as imagine (and plan for) your friendship dreamscape as it may unfold across all the tomorrows to come. It's a really useful journey and one we think you're going to love, but here at the outset we think it's wise to tell you that we're going to get up in your business. Like, way, *way* up in there. We're going to do for you what we wish someone had done for us, back when we were fumbling our way through friendship's doldrums, losing hope like sand through a sieve.

Our promise to you is that if you will stick with these lessons in their entirety, you will find it vastly easier to establish friendships, you will do a much better job maintaining the friendships you've got, and you will feel happier and more hopeful about this "friendship thing" being for you. Fair enough?

We think so, too.

* * *

A quick note about the layout of this guide, and then we'll turn you loose to begin. You can work through these lessons alone or in a group; either way, consider these two pro tips for setting yourself up for success:

1. If it's possible for you to secure a copy of the book that this study is based on—*I'll Be There, But I'll Be Wearing Sweatpants,* (Thomas Nelson 2022)—do so. Read the chapter each lesson is based on before completing that portion of this workbook.

2. If you choose to work through this content in a group setting—with friends, neighbors, family members, work colleagues, etc.—we strongly

recommend completing each lesson on your own prior to the group meeting when that lesson will be discussed. Many of the questions/ prompts are highly personal in nature, and many require significant thought. Best to have your thoughts already thunk (creative spelling) and logged before feeling pressed to share them in a full group.

While we're on the topic of group discussion, you'll notice that each lesson contains four main parts:

1. "Get Going" :: The lesson overview and one setup question to whet your appetite for the content to come.
2. "Catch Your Breath" :: An opportunity to take one to two minutes in silence before working through the discussion questions.
3. "Dive Deep" :: Discussion questions to consider and respond to.
4. "What Now?" :: An action item or two to help you practice what you learned before convening for the next lesson.

If you structure your group time according to a ninety-minute lesson, then you might divide your time this way:

Get Going: 10 minutes

Catch Your Breath: 5 minutes

Dive Deep: 50 minutes

What Now?: 25 minutes

We wish you well on your friendship journey! Every minute you devote to the process of gathering sisters to your side and also becoming a better friend will pay huge dividends for you. We cheer you on as you begin. To friendship! To friendship, for sure.

1

When You Really Need a Friend (Yeah, Us Too)

We want to be known. We want to be seen. We want to be loved as we are, where we are, with what we have.

Based on Chapter 1

Jess and Amy

GET GOING

"I'll be there."

Isn't it always a total relief to hear those three words? Whether they are said in response to an invitation you sent to a gathering, an everyday request for participation, or a middle-of-the-night cry for help, there's nothing quite as comforting as hearing someone say to you that you don't need to fret, that you won't be alone, that *they'll for sure be there.*

Nobody wants to do life alone. Or we should say, nobody wants to do *all* of life alone. At some point, we all long for another person to witness our lives—to share a laugh, to help shoulder a burden, to celebrate a massive achievement, to revisit a momentous experience, to dive into a giant bowl of steaming-hot queso from that beloved restaurant with us.

True for you? When do you most crave true friendship? When you're ridiculously happy? Super-sad? Up to your eyeballs in stress? Some other time? Do tell . . .

CATCH YOUR BREATH

Before moving on, take a moment to silently consider your answer to the last question. Why do you suppose you crave true friendship at that time? What needs do you suspect true friendship might fill in your life that are going unfulfilled today?

DIVE DEEP

One of the occupational hazards of writing a book about friendship is you start thinking about friendship all. the. time. As in, for two years straight, all you think about is this singular topic. We have *thoughts* about friendship, I'm telling you. And one of them is what the term even means. So, right from the top, let's get some definitional work out of the way.

How would you define *friendship*? In other words:

- What does it mean to "have a friend"?
- What does it *not* mean?
- How do you know when an acquaintance has become a friend?

When we talk about friendship, as we said in the book, "*We're talking about the kind of friendship that gets raw and gritty. The kind of friendship that is built for real life and running errands. The kind of friendship that is safe for big feelings, deep secrets, and laughing so hard you snort. The kind of friendship that stays through sickness, health, anxiety, and announcements like, "Hey, something is hanging out of your nose.*"

Anything in our definition stand out to you? If so, what?

Describe a season of life when you enjoyed this kind of real, raw, no-holds-barred connection with a friend or friend group.

- Where were you, and who were you with?
- What dynamics were in play?

- What types of experiences did you share?

What benefits showed up in your life during or after that season, because of knowing and being known by a true friend?

- ◯ Confidence
- ◯ Peace
- ◯ Strength
- ◯ Companionship
- ◯ Personal growth
- ◯ Emotional growth
- ◯ Spiritual growth
- ◯ Secondary friendships
- ◯ Hope
- ◯ Comfort
- ◯ Joy
- ◯ Less stress/anxiety
- ◯ Less loneliness
- ◯ Creativity
- ◯ Effectiveness
- ◯ Efficiency
- ◯ Feeling seen
- ◯ Feeling known
- ◯ Feeling cared for
- ◯ Feeling loved
- ◯ Learned to trust
- ◯ Learned to laugh
- ◯ Learned to communicate
- ◯ Learned to resolve conflict
- ◯ Learned about God
- ◯ Learned to love
- ◯ Something else:

How does that season of life compare with the relational season you're in now? How have things changed for you, on the friendship front? How have they stayed the same?

> We've done the obligatory half-laughs. We've eaten food we hated, and we've tried for so long just to belong somewhere—anywhere—and now, we just want to be with people who feel comfortable. We want friendships that feel secure and made to last.

If you could twinkle your nose and alter your current friendship situation, what circumstances would you want to see unfold? What magic do you wish you could unleash on your present relational reality?

* * *

If you're anything like us, seeing that desired state written out in your own handwriting can cause your heart to sink a little: *Will I ever have real friends? Will my current reality ever really change? Is there any hope for me?*

We posed those exact questions and worked like crazy to get them answered, which is how we can tell you with complete confidence that if you stay this course, you *will* have real friends, and that your reality can *absolutely* change, and that there is so, so much hope for us all. As a matter of fact, we wrote an entire book to prove these things to you, so if you haven't read it yet, well, what are you waiting for? It's good! (It's at least *pretty* good. We trust you'll think so.)

We'll talk more in the lessons to come about exactly how to get your reality to look more and more like your friendship dreamscape, but for now, let's get our expectations properly set for what lies ahead. As we noted in chapter 1, previous generations made time for each other. Friendship didn't "just happen." Women got together on a regular basis. They cooked together. They cleaned together. They shopped together. They worshipped God together. They stopped by for a "visit." They shamelessly stuck their noses into each other's business and refused to apologize for it. They tattled on each other's kids. They looked out for their own. They pushed pause on other stuff, just to have time to be with their friends.

They said yes.

They showed up.

They spoke up.

They shared what they had.

They asked the question, and the question after that.

They forgave.

Most importantly, they kept at it, over time.

We bring all this up because despite all the advances in technology that have been made across the years, relationships that are worth their linked arms and private jokes still require a whole lot of action verbs. They still require a significant investment of time and energy and heart. They still demand to be tended to, to be fought for, to be prized.

Just curious: How do you feel about the audacity of friendship to require so much of us? In your previous friendships, have you found these demands to be true?

WHAT NOW?

There is an upside to this whole dynamic, which we'd like to draw your attention to now: While it is true that finding and maintaining true friendships will require much of us, they return to us vastly more.

> Keep investing in friendship. Keep watering. Keep loving. Keep being reliable and consistent. It will be worth it. It will be worth it every time.

Take another look at the benefits you noted on the previous page, during or after that season of friendship you said you enjoyed. What would you say were the top three investments you made during that season? What were the top three returns? Spend a few minutes calling up those memories in your mind's eye, and then jot down your recollections on the grid below.

A BELOVED FRIENDSHIP

THE HARD STUFF: INVESTMENTS I MADE	THE GOOD STUFF: BENEFITS I ENJOYED
1.	1.
2.	2.
3.	3.

In the end, were those investments worth it? Any encouragement your *previous* self would offer to your *current* self, regarding the value of throwing ourselves fully into the work of finding and keeping good friends?

As we get underway, what fears or insecurities do you think might get in the way of your friendship-building efforts?

In case you haven't committed our entire book to memory just yet, let us remind you that the whole reason we wrote that book, which we divulged in chapter 1, was because we both were tired of being nearly debilitated by fear and insecurity on the relational front.

We were *just sure* that life had overlooked and forgotten us, that we were destined to be lonely for the rest of our days.

We *just knew* that we were the problem, that *we* were the colossal fails.

We both were stuck—there's no other way to put it. We were stuck with no way to move ahead.

The one glimmer of hope for us was that we truly had nothing to lose. When you're staring up at the belly of the bottom of things, there's no way to go but up. And so we decided that we might as well give the whole friendship quest a try. We would devote our best thoughts and prayers and actions to the singular goal of *not doing life alone*. And we would see where that devotion would take us.

You can imagine our shock when it worked.

It worked.

Imperfectly, but still.

So, those fears and insecurities that you don't quite know what to do with? We'll get to those. We'll address those. We'll work around those. We'll put those things in your relational rearview mirror. Swear.

Stick with us, deal? We're going places.

Best of all? We're going there *together*.

When You're Alone and It All Kinda Sucks

Friendship is hard, and it's messy.

Based on Chapter 2

Amy

GET GOING

Adulting is hard. Can I get an amen? Remember the day you realized that if your car was going to have a full tank, *you* were going to have to stop and get gas? And if your bills were going to get handled, *you* were going to have to pay them? And if your clothes were going to get clean, you were going to have to do laundry? Such an unwelcomed wakeup call, isn't it, this thing called becoming an adult?

And then there's friendship. While there was a time long, long ago when you could just show up in some age-appropriate setting—

a preschool classroom, a neighborhood, a ballet class, a sports team, a high-school homeroom, a dorm's dining hall—and make friends, cultivating friendship in adulthood takes *work*. Like, *lots* of work.

Are you feeling this reality these days? How would you describe your current friendship dynamic? More work, or more recess? More pain, or more joy? More trick, or more treat?

I said in chapter 2 that one of the problems with adult friendships is that finding people is so exhausting. It takes so long to break them in! And yet when we let ourselves be held back from forging ahead in friendship, we settle for outright loneliness.

CATCH YOUR BREATH

Take a moment to sit silently with your answer to the previous question. Are you happy with the truth of your current friendship landscape? If yes, what's making it work so well? If not, why not? What do you wish were true that just isn't the case today?

DIVE DEEP

When do you notice the pangs of loneliness? What situations bring a lonely sensation to the surface for you? Tick any of the following options, and/or add a few of your own.

- ○ You walk into a room and don't recognize a single face.

- A good friendship ends. The friend moves away. Circumstances shift. Things change.
- You can't find a good friendship in the first place.
- Your life feels like it's falling apart.
- You win, and there's nobody to celebrate with.
- You look up and realize that you're dripping with acquaintances but can't name a single close friend.
- ______
- ______
- ______

How do you generally cope with your loneliness? Which comforts do you turn to, and how effectively do they help?

In the last few decades, the number of Americans who believe they don't have any close friends has nearly tripled. Even sadder, according to data from the General Social Survey, when people are asked how many confidants they have, the most common answer is none.

Something inside of us knows that loneliness is not a sustainable strategy for getting through life. And yet that breaking-in period of adult friendships can just be the *worst*. We don't know how to make an introduction. We don't know what to say. We don't know what to do. We don't know how to proceed. We don't want to come across as stalkerish. And so we stay put—all alone.

What gives? Why are adult friendships so weird? Why is it so hard to make and keep good friends?

You and I both have weird-friend stories. (Please tell me you have them, too?) I promise I'm not asking you to note a few of them here to torture you. But still: I'm asking you to note them. Think back on a few of the weird-friend situations you've been in. The time when you unintentionally offended someone within the first three minutes of knowing her. The time when things got sideways early on and only got worse from there. The time when you thought you were headed in a good direction, only to discover things weren't what they appeared to be.

What friendship weirdness still messes with you today? What situations have you faced firsthand, in your efforts to make new friends?

1.

2.

3.

4.

5.

The method to my madness in asking you to replay some of these less-desirable reels is that regardless of how sucky the start, *no effort toward genuine friendship is ever made in vain*. There is always a realization to make, a lesson to learn, a distinction to catalog, an aha to glean. True? True.

Think back on the situations you noted in the previous question. What did you learn from each of them? Complete the sentence starters below.

Because I faced ______________________________,
I learned ______________________________.

Because I faced ______________________________,
I learned ______________________________.

Because I faced ______________________________,
I learned ______________________________.

Because I faced ______________________________,
I learned ______________________________.

Because I faced ______________________________,
I learned ______________________________.

The thing is, when you and I take all that we've learned from all that we've experienced into the next friendship, that friendship stands a better chance at success. So, yeah, we can let the old ghosts haunt us interminably and keep us from ever trying again. But equally true is that instead of being haunted, we can be heartened. We can remember that *connected* is how we're made to live.

> When we live connected to other people, we grow stronger.
>
> When we live connected to other people, we grow braver.
>
> When we live connected to other people, we build better things.
>
> When we live connected to other people, we are more helpful.

When we live connected to other people, we are happier.

When we live connected to other people, we more frequently *light up the dark*.

Let me ask you: If you and I were sitting across from each other, a bowl of thick, creamy queso and a giant basket of tortilla chips between us, and I asked you to rattle off your top-ten list of favorite memories from your life so far, what would you say?

Go ahead. Give it a whirl. (If coming up with your *all-time top ten* is too intimidating, then how about ten *favorite* memories? Ten *pretty good* memories? Ten times life didn't suck?) Ready, set, write:

1.

2.

3.

4.

5.

6.

7.

8.

9.

10.

Now, go back to that list and circle the ones that feature you by yourself, all alone.

I'll wait.

How many did you circle? I'm guessing somewhere around . . . none?

Life is meant to be lived connected. To people. To sisters. To *friends.*

* * *

You know that I'm a Jesus-girl through and through, and one of the things that keeps me coming back to the (weird, awkward, awful, sometimes-embarrassing) process of making and keeping friends is that I have noticed a trend in my life: Whenever I grow in my relationship with God, I long to grow in my relationships with the people he creates and loves. As I realize with fresh awareness how good he has been to me, I can't help but want to be good to the girls in my life. As I see how deeply he loves me, it's like I start craving someone to love.

How do you connect with this idea that you, too, are divinely seen and loved?

We don't crave connection because we are doing life wrong. We crave connection because, to the depths of our DNA, that's how we were built. We were built to be together and to love together and to laugh together and to experience life together.

Do you think it's possible to love people without loving God? What about the inverse? Can you love God without loving the people he has made?

WHAT NOW?

Regardless of what you've been through on the friendship front, and of how things are looking for you today, my promise to you is that you were not only *made* for friendship, but also that sturdy friendships can be yours. You don't have to believe me just yet. In this early stage of our journey together, you can borrow my belief. All I'm asking you to do is to *act* like you believe. I'm asking you to trust Jess and me not to lead you astray. I'm asking you to step out in faith. (Baby-stepping is totally fine.)

> Baby steps are just the right speed for success.

All right. Here goes. Your (baby) step for this week is to pick at least one of the (terrifying! disconcerting! uncomfortable! unpredictable!) actions below to complete before you start lesson three. I'm here for you. I've got you. More importantly, *you've got this.*

- ○ Show up, even though you really, really want to stay home.
- ○ Extend the invitation you so wish you could receive.

- Answer the call.
- Reply (truthfully) to the text right away.
- Remember—and celebrate—the birthday.
- Swallow your pride. Let what goes without saying go without saying.

Are you sweating, just *reading* that list? Been there, done that, too. My best advice is to gather your scared, sweaty self together and get going on nailing that list.

When You Can't Amazon Prime Your Friendships

Life is too beautiful and too terrible not to do it with people who truly know and love us.

Based on Chapter 3

Jess

GET GOING

Time. Finding someone who actually has enough of it is like spotting a unicorn in the wild. *Nobody* has enough time. Ask around, and the first thing most people will tell you in response to your saying, "Hey, how are you doing!" is some version of, "Fine! Busy. But fine. Did I mention busy?"

Have you ever wondered what we're all so busy doing?

Let's start with you. Not to be crass, but what *are* you so busy doing?

CATCH YOUR BREATH

Can you spare sixty seconds? I want to invite you to think about your answer here, the answer to what you're so busy doing. How does your response line up with your values? In other words, regarding how you're spending your time these days, how close are you to being the person you say you want to be?

DIVE DEEP

If you're like me, you can't even find time to sweep the crumbs off the kitchen floor that have been there since Taco Tuesday . . . three weeks ago. Finding time to cultivate friendships? Ha. Or more the case: *Hahahahaha*! Who has time for that?

And yet in the same way that we sometimes mysteriously, miraculously find time to know every plot point of every episode of *Bridgerton* at all times, as we start to see the importance of sisters in our day-to-day lives, we'll start carving out time for them, too.

What obligations or activities do you suspect might have to take a back seat for a while—a month, a year, the next five decades?—if you were to start prioritizing reaching out to, encouraging, and engaging with friends?

- ○ ______________________________
- ○ ______________________________
- ○ ______________________________

Who in your life right now do you wish you could start with? Who do you wish you could stop being acquaintances—or even *strangers*—with and start a friendship with them?

Hang onto those names as you work through this lesson and the lessons to come. I'm willing to bet that those people are on your heart and mind for a reason. Let's see if we can sort out why that is.

* * *

While it's true that it takes a long time to make old friends, I can't think of many things in this life that are better than old friendships that still sing. Think about your own life . . . your current friendship landscape, if you will.

Describe a time when you've really "been there" for a friend. Something big went down, you got the text or the call, you said yes, and you actually showed up for her. What were the circumstances? What do you remember about the turn of events?

Now the fun part. If I asked you to rewind that relationship to the very beginning, what shared experiences between you and that friend qualified you to be there for her that day? Jot down as many as you can recall.

There is always a story between a friendship's first memory and "being there" for a friend. There are always a *thousand* stories, truth be told. Friendship is like that, unfolding and evolving and deepening over time—you know, that thing that we don't seem to have.

Realizing you don't have old friends is like realizing you don't have full-grown trees in your yard. You don't want a sapling. A sapling doesn't do anything. In fact, you have to water and care for a sapling. A sapling takes time, and you don't have time. What you really want is to be able to sit and drink lemonade in the shade of its giant branches, right this very minute. You demand the comfort only a large trunk and leaves can provide, and you don't want to wait for something to grow.

Question for you: If time weren't an issue, what types of friendship experiences do you wish you could share with someone?

What adventures would you embark on, what stores would you hit, what classes would you take, what fun things would you learn, what habits would you form with someone, if you only had time for a friend?

WHAT NOW?

It's tempting to buy into the belief that the old friends we have today just magically appeared out of thin air, but the reality is that every friendship begins with one person reaching out to another, asking a question, making an invitation, risking looking ridiculous, and working like crazy at being a friend.

Could you be that "one person" today?

What could you say or do today that would convey to a potential friend some pretty powerful messages:

- "I see you."
- "I value you."
- "I am interested in knowing you better."
- "I am prepared to invest in your life . . . for real."

For the record, who *doesn't* like to hear these things? You and I both like to know that someone out there sees us and values us and finds us interesting, don't we?

Yeah. Rhetorical question, if ever there were one.

So, with that reality in mind, let's hit that question once more: What could you say or do today to convey life-giving messages such as those? Tick the ideas below that resonate most with you and/or invent a few of your own.

- ○ Text a kind word to a friend.
- ○ Set up a monthly girls' night out with a few people you'd love to know better.

- Ask a friend how she's doing regarding a situation you know she's dealing with. Then, ask the next question after that. How can you help? What burden can you help bear? How might you pray for her? When is a good time for you to check in again?
- Initiate a Facetime call with a friend who lives far away.
- Strike up a conversation with someone you don't know but who catches your attention for some reason.
- Get two of something fun or functional today—a latte, a great-smelling candle, a box of brownie mix, a jumbo package of toilet paper?—and share with a neighbor or friend.
- ______________________________
- ______________________________

What do you think the effect could be of incorporating simple—and yeah, sometimes random—acts of kindness into your set of daily to-do's? How might your friendship circle expand? How might your current friendships grow?

4

When Insecurity Reigns Supreme

Keep your heart open. Keep being good to others. Live fierce and love free. Believe. Breathe. And have a good time.

Based on Chapter 4

Amy

GET GOING

Who we are and how we're feeling on the inside is often a real contrast to who people believe us to be—and how they think we're doing—on the outside. Have you ever noticed this? For example, maybe you're a frenetic person who always has a thousand plates spinning and is forever stressing about what's being left undone on your to-do list. A friend writes in a birthday card to you, "You have such a peaceful presence," and you can't help but laugh.

Either she doesn't know the real you, or you have gotten so good at faking peacefulness that even your close friends are fooled.

Or maybe you're dangerously close to bankruptcy because you can't seem to stop buying trendy clothes and leasing the latest model of the car you just can't live without. A friend says, "I should have you help me learn how to budget better. You *always* have money for new stuff."

How is it she doesn't know that you're faking it? How can her perception of you be so far from what's real?

Here's another one: Somehow, despite your longstanding disdain for vegetables, you and your friend always wind up at the same vegan restaurant at the front of your neighborhood when you grab dinner together. She thinks you *love* this place. In reality, you just can't deal. What gives? Why is her view so far from the truth?

How well do your friends know you? Would they say you're orderly or a disaster? Would they say you're outgoing or shy? Would they say you're efficient or laid back? Would they say you're more of a large-gathering person or someone who prefers intimate connection every time? Who would your friends say that you are? And would their perceptions of you actually be true?

CATCH YOUR BREATH

Before we plow ahead, sit with that last answer a sec. Two questions come to mind that I'd like you to answer for yourself:

1. How did your friends come to the perceptions they hold of you?
2. How well do you *want* to be known by your friends?

DIVE DEEP

On this subject of being known well by friends, one thing that always surprises me is discovering *just how many of us* struggle with insecurity. We work hard to look on the outside like we have it all together, while on the inside we're dying a thousand deaths every time we leave our house. Crazy, right?

> Insecurity will wreak havoc on your mental health, your work, your goals. It will sneak in there and mess up your marriage, your relationships, the way you see yourself in the mirror, the way you sleep. You'll start seeing yourself as someone who wasn't created with a purpose, and you'll start seeing nothing but a mess.

Why do you think it's hard for so many of us to admit to a friend when we feel incapable or unattractive or weak?

What do you suppose is the connection between having people in your life who *truly know you* and experiencing life as someone who is unflinchingly secure?

I told you that a primary way my insecurity shows up in my life is by my seeming inability to receive a compliment with grace. Something in me just *doesn't buy* that a person could think well of me. Terrible way to go through life, right? And yet deflecting affirming comments is hardly the only way that insecurity can manifest itself, which brings me to the subject of *you*.

When insecurity rears its head in your life, what form does it generally take?

- ○ "I neglect to voice my opinion."
- ○ "I go along to get along, even when people are going the wrong way."
- ○ "I fish for compliments."
- ○ "I'm overly defensive in conversation."
- ○ "I assume everyone is mad at me or doesn't like me or doesn't want to include me in their plans."
- ○ "I feel forever on the outside of what everyone else is up to."
- ○ "I come across as needy, asking way too many questions about why someone didn't respond to my text."
- ○ Something else:

It may be hard to believe, but at the core of *every* manifestation of insecurity is our four-letter enemy, *fear*. Whenever you and I settle for playing it small, fear is what's steering our wheel.

Peek back at the answer you gave to the previous question. Which fear do you suspect is most often motivating that particular manifestation of insecurity?

- ○ Fear of rejection.
- ○ Fear of being left out.
- ○ Fear of being unliked.
- ○ Fear of being unlikeable.
- ○ Fear of saying the wrong thing.
- ○ Fear of doing the wrong thing.
- ○ Fear of being gossiped about.
- ○ Fear of offending someone.
- ○ Fear of not being enough.
- ○ Fear that friendship just isn't for you.

So, what's the problem with letting fear run roughshod over our lives? For starters, it's tough to be friends with someone who is paralyzed by fear. People love friends who are consistent. Who show up for them when they say that they will. Who can laugh at the everyday struggles of life. Who are steady when storms erupt. Of course, we're all going to experience a few dips here and there, times when the rug absolutely gets yanked from under our feet and we find ourselves splatted facedown in the muck. But when that splatted state has no end in sight? Well, that's a difficult thing to accept.

When have you seen a "splatted state" go on too long—either in your own life or in the life of someone you love? What were the circumstances involved, and what happened as a result?

So, what do you do when you're struggling with fear and insecurity and can't seem to get unstuck? I've been there! And I can help.

For way too long, I believed the lie that insecurity and humility were two sides of the very same coin. In fact, insecurity is humility's opposite: What's possible when we're feeling insecure is completely *impossible* when humility is guiding our steps.

Let me give you a few distinctions that have helped me along the way.

INSECURITY VS. HUMILITY

CATEGORY	THE WAY OF INSECURITY	THE WAY OF HUMILITY
Focus:	Self.	Others.
Goal:	Finding the bad in us.	Finding the good in other people.
Fuel:	Works for love.	Works from love.
Message:	"You have design flaws."	"You have quirks, like everyone."
M.O.:	Impress others.	Welcome others in.
Style:	Passive aggression.	Authenticity.
Key Question:	"Can you help me?"	"Can I help?"
Battle Cry:	"Cling or die!"	"Connect or die!"

We could keep coming up with categories that delineate insecurity from humility, but our point would be the same: These two subjects can't be any more diverse! They live at opposite ends of every spectrum, and when they see each other, they *run*.

Let me prove it to you using your own life as our example. In the space below, I'd like you to form two lists, one that is centered on insecurity, and one with humility at its core. First, to insecurity's rundown. As quickly as possible, fill in the bullet-point list below with fixes to every one of your flaws. Need to drop ten pounds to reach your goal weight? Then "lose weight" goes on the list. Sick of never finishing a book you start? "Finish a book" goes on your list. Weary of bailing out of girls' night every time? Put "say yes" on your list. Ready to throw something across the room every time you catch sight of the innards of your hall closet? "Organize closet" gets a bullet point.

Got the gist of how to make your first list? Ready, set, *write.*

- ○ ______________________
- ○ ______________________
- ○ ______________________
- ○ ______________________
- ○ ______________________
- ○ ______________________
- ○ ______________________
- ○ ______________________
- ○ ______________________
- ○ ______________________
- ○ ______________________
- ○ ______________________
- ○ ______________________
- ○ ______________________
- ○ ______________________
- ○ ______________________
- ○ ______________________
- ○ ______________________
- ○ ______________________
- ○ ______________________
- ○ ______________________
- ○ ______________________
- ○ ______________________
- ○ ______________________

How do you feel right now, if I may ask? What emotions rose to the surface for you, as you made your way through your list?

Next, to humility's list. This one is so much happier, I promise! Hang with me, and you'll see. From this moment forward, whenever you think about humility, I want two ideas to pop into your head. Here they are:

1. Like self.

2. Get over self.

That's it! Humility is simply choosing to *like ourselves*—which means accepting who we are, for what we are, and where we are at this moment in time—and *get over ourselves* so that we can focus on someone else. I even made you a pretty picture, in case that's easier for you to understand. The idea is that as we practice *liking* ourselves, we are better able to *get over* ourselves and look for opportunities to show up for our friends. And as we engage with and encourage and experience life with our friends, guess what happens? We feel better about ourselves. In this way, getting over ourselves repositions us for liking ourselves all over again. Brilliant! I'm telling you: Humility cures insecurity, every. single. time.

Insecurity need not have its way in your life.

* * *

Ready to make that "humility" list? Let's give it a try. On the left, note all the things you like about yourself. Do you always have a witty opening line that makes people feel seen and included and adored? Are you ridiculously good at procuring the *perfect* birthday gift? Are your leg muscles crazy strong? Do you get compliments on your stunning eyes or infectious laugh? Are you rocking homeschooling these days?

That's the left side. Now, to the right.

In the righthand column, list all the things that come to mind that you could do for a friend, if time and money weren't a concern.

Left side: Things you like about yourself. Right side: Ways you could love or serve a friend. All set? Begin.

Things I Like About Me	Ways I Could Love or Serve a Friend
○ ______	○ ______
○ ______	○ ______
○ ______	○ ______
○ ______	○ ______
○ ______	○ ______
○ ______	○ ______
○ ______	○ ______
○ ______	○ ______
○ ______	○ ______
○ ______	○ ______
○ ______	○ ______
○ ______	○ ______

> I liked myself enough to get over myself, and when I got over myself, it allowed me to focus on everyone around me, which is the single greatest key to connection.

It may be obvious to you that when we refuse to intentionally like ourselves—and by definition then get over ourselves—another sequence takes hold: We hate ourselves, so we can't get over ourselves, which makes us hate ourselves even more. Trust me: That's not who we want to be. We can't sustain authentic friendship until we can reach out to other people and love them well.

But oh, the beauty that unfolds when we do. After all, who doesn't long to be accepted and affirmed and admired and adored? We all love all these things. And when you start this cycle, others will follow. Others will choose humility, too.

WHAT NOW?

You will be known for something someday. And as it relates to our topic at hand, you will either be known as someone who was needy and clingy and down on herself all the time, or else you will be known as someone who believed the best—about herself, about others, about life.

Just wondering, which will it be?

- ◯ I will be known as the insecure one.
- ◯ I will be known as the humble one.

Amazing, right? We get to choose.

If you chose wisely—in this case, the humble one—then this next part's for you: A whole slew of get-going ideas.

Ways to Start *Liking and Getting Over* Yourself

- ◯ **Get to know yourself better.** Take a few personality tests, so that you can better understand how you tick. For now, pay attention only to the upside of your personality. What is *fantastic* about your type?
- ◯ **Discover your spiritual gifts.** Online assessments abound, but they all lead to pretty much the same handful of gifts. What is yours, and why is it useful, in the broader world in which you live?

- **See a counselor.** If you're in need of help, get help! Pay for a friend until you can be a good friend, I say. No shame whatsoever in that.
- **Interrupt your negative thoughts.** Whenever you feel yourself starting to veer off-course into insecurity territory, pause what you're doing and remind yourself that you are your first best friend. If you wouldn't say something to your very best friend, then refuse to say it to yourself.
- **Write a self-affirming letter.** And tuck it somewhere that you'll frequently see. Tell yourself what is lovely about you. Remind yourself what God says about you. (See Ephesians 2:8–10 and Psalm 139, for starters.) Hold fast to what is true of you instead of being led astray by lies.

When You're Pretty Sure You've Been Duped

We can have a billion people admire us, but that will never fill the same need as having even just one person truly love us.

Based on Chapter 5

Jess

GET GOING

We ended the last lesson talking about lies we're prone to believe, which is the perfect segue into this lesson's topic: Still. more. lies. It can feel frustrating to go through life so vulnerable to untruth, can't it? And yet if there's one thing I've learned along the way, it's that when you've been heading in the wrong direction for so long, it can take a fair amount of effort to get where you were hoping to go.

That's how it is with accepting ourselves and showing up authentically in the friendships we seek: Until we drop the lies we've been holding fast to, our arms are too full to welcome truth in. Cue this lesson. Let the dropping officially begin.

Can you relate? When have you let an untruth about you—something someone said about you, something you vowed was true about yourself—live in your mind and heart far too long? What was the lie, and why did you keep it close? What damage did it do?

CATCH YOUR BREATH

If you're a spiritually-inclined person, take a moment to pray a simple prayer asking God to expose the lies you've been believing and to help you discern the truth.

DIVE DEEP

A little something different, this time around. For the balance of this lesson, you are cordially invited to scrutinize some lies you may have believed—about yourself and about friendship—along the way. Consider following these simple steps, if you will:

1. Read the lie and my summary of the lie.

2. On the lines below the lie, jot down the gist of the lie using your own words and/or an example from your life of the lie at work.
3. Rate on the dot scale provided how destructive the lie has been in your life—one dot for not so much, five dots for, "Uh, quit reading my mail."

After we've covered all ten lies, stick around to work through the process that follows, which will help you drop your most pernicious lies once and for all and practice clinging to truth.

Lie #1: *We have to be impressive to have friends.*

This lie tries to sell us on the belief that if we are just pretty enough, smart enough, thin enough, funny enough, and followed by enough of the right people online, we'll be found acceptable. We'll qualify for having friends.

Define it: What words would you put to this lie?

Rate it: How destructive has this lie been in your life? ○ ○ ○ ○ ○

Lie #2: *Popularity = Connection.*

This lie peddles the assumption that the more *likes* you rack up—literally, on social media, or figuratively, in everyday life—the more substantive friendships you enjoy.

Define it: What words would you put to this lie?

Rate it: How destructive has this lie been in your life? ○ ○ ○ ○ ○

Lie #3: *You must filter your mess out of the picture.*

This lie says, "Get your junk—the actual mess in the background of the shot you just posted as well as the unfinished business lurking in your heart—cleaned up, or else you're always going to be lacking friends."

Define it: What words would you put to this lie?

Rate it: How destructive has this lie been in your life? ○ ○ ○ ○ ○

Lie #4: *Friends should understand when you go MIA.*

Ready for this one? This lie makes us think that we can be flaky, unkind, unpredictable, or lazy in our friendships and still have those friends pursue us. It says, "Hey, you can be too busy for your friends and still have deep friendships. No problem at all, whatsoever."

Define it: What words would you put to this lie?

Rate it: How destructive has this lie been in your life? ○ ○ ○ ○ ○

Lie #5: *It's all about self-care.*

This lie keeps us focused on what we need instead of looking up every once in a while to see how we might show up for a friend. "You can love someone without ever serving her"—that's the mantra of this lie.

Define it: What words would you put to this lie?

Rate it: How destructive has this lie been in your life? ○ ○ ○ ○ ○

Lie #6: *Friendship is an extra, not a necessity.*

This lie reinforces the idea that while conversation and connection and intimacy with friends are nice to have, they're not essential to a life well-lived.

Define it: What words would you put to this lie?

Rate it: How destructive has this lie been in your life? ○ ○ ○ ○ ○

Lie #7: *Friendship is impossible.*

I know far too many women who have *still* not dropped this lie. It's the lie that convinces us that adults just don't have friends. Friendship cannot happen, it will not happen . . . and it *especially* won't happen for you.

Define it: What words would you put to this lie?

Rate it: How destructive has this lie been in your life? ○ ○ ○ ○ ○

Lie #8: *Friendship just "happens."*

"You don't need to do anything to find friendship," this lie says. "No need to reach out. To say hey. To make an invitation. To ask a meaningful question. Nah, just keep on keepin' on, doing your thing. Friendship will show up when it's ready."

Define it: What words would you put to this lie?

Rate it: How destructive has this lie been in your life? ○ ○ ○ ○ ○

Lie #9: *Saying "bye, girl" is the norm.*

This lie? It will have you believing in no time that friendships once attained will never need to be fought for. If they fade? Well, then so be it. Must be time to move on.

Define it: What words would you put to this lie?

Rate it: How destructive has this lie been in your life? ○ ○ ○ ○ ○

Lie #10: *You're the only one without good friends.*

"Everyone is hanging out, having a ball, and probably wearing matching sweatshirts without you." That's what this lie would have you believe. "*Eeeeveryone* has found their people. *Eeeeveryone* has found their tribe. *Eeeeveryone* is thriving in friendships. Everyone, that is, but you."

Define it: What words would you put to this lie?

Rate it: How destructive has this lie been in your life? ○ ○ ○ ○ ○

WHAT NOW?

Evil little suckers, aren't they? Those lies are on a mission to *kill*. And yet despite the damage they've surely wreaked in your life, I come bearing good news today. You can drag those lies—each and every one of them—into the blazing light of day. You can see them for what they are. You can drop them like the latte you were trying to balance on a stack of books. And you can choose to start walking in the truth.

I'm going to show you how to work through this progression using one of the lies as a case-in-point, but know that if you are struggling with believing *multiple* lies, the system will work the same for each one.

First things first, of the ten lies I introduced in the book and revisited in this guide, which did you rate the highest in its destructive effect? (If you had several lies that landed the same score, pick one of them for this exercise.)

- ○ **Lie #1:** We have to be impressive to have friends.
- ○ **Lie #2:** Popularity = Connection.
- ○ **Lie #3:** You must filter your mess out of the picture.
- ○ **Lie #4:** Friends should understand when you go MIA.
- ○ **Lie #5:** It's all about self-care.
- ○ **Lie #6:** Friendship is an extra, not a necessity.
- ○ **Lie #7:** Friendship is impossible.
- ○ **Lie #8:** Friendship just "happens."
- ○ **Lie #9:** Saying "bye, girl" is the norm.
- ○ **Lie #10:** You're the only one without good friends.

Do you have the lie you want to dispel at the top of your mind? Write it again in the space below.

Second, capture in a few sentences the situation in your life that persuaded you to believe that lie. What were the circumstances? Who was involved? What turn of events unfolded? How did your heart get hurt?

Third, try to recollect how believing that lie made you behave. What did you say (or not say)? What did you do (or not do)? How did accepting that lie as fact dictate how you responded?

Fourth—and this is key—write down the opposite of the lie you believed. For example, if you chose the lie, "Friendship is impossible," you would write, "Friendship is *possible.*" If you chose, "Friends should understand when you go MIA," you would write something like, "Friends *shouldn't be expected* to understand when I go MIA." Write your lie's opposite on the line below.

Now, here's the hard part. Once you have that opposite written down, choose to live as though it is true. (Which ought to be easy, because guess what? It is.)

Choose to live as though it is true.

Choose to drop the lie you've been believing and pick up truth instead. Write it on a sticky note and put it on the mirror in your bathroom if you must, but get that truth into your mind. And into your heart. And into your way of friending. Start operating from the truth.

As we talked about in the last lesson, untangle yourself from living a lie so that you can start *liking yourself* again. Quit handing over your confidence to the enemy of your soul. Learn the truth. Lean on the truth. Live from a place of truthfulness in every relationship you have. You know the words of John 8:32 as well as I do: "The truth will set you free."

Choose today to live free—that's it.

Choose today to live free.

6

When You Wonder Why No One Likes You

For some people, you are going to be too salty, and for others, you're going to be too sweet. For some, you will be too bold, and for others, you won't have nearly enough flavor. You will be both too much and not enough for some people's taste buds, and that's okay.

Based on Chapter 6

Amy

GET GOING

Sometimes friendship is a balm, and sometimes friendship is the reason we need a balm in the first place. Funny how life works, yes? The thing that helps us and heartens us and fills us with hope for the days ahead can also be the very thing that punches us right in the gut.

Friendship can be super!

And yep, friendship can be hard. For me, this generally has to do with someone not liking me. Now, your turn:

When is friendship hardest for you?

CATCH YOUR BREATH

Before you get going on the deep dive, spend a few minutes thinking about the "hards" you've had to face. You surely see the other person's role in the hard. Do you also see the role that you played?

DIVE DEEP

As I said, one of the hardest things about friendship I've dealt with is that awful realization that despite your most charming efforts, some people just aren't going to like you. You! With all your wonderful attributes! The injustice of it all, right?

"If they only *knew* us," we're prone to thinking. And yet, nope, they probably still wouldn't budge. Try as you might, you're just not going to jibe with everyone. And in case this provides a smidge of encouragement, not everyone will jibe with *you*.

This is the case, I've come to realize, because we all have a fairly big thing. My thing, as I've so generously disclosed already, is that I pretty much need all people to be pleased with me at all times and in all ways. (Is that too much to ask??) I know other people whose thing is perfectionism. As in, lack of excellence? They just can't deal. I know people whose thing is organization. And people whose thing is leap-frogging over all rational thought to get to the worst-case scenario in a jiffy.

If I were sitting across from you right now, I'd lean in and grin and whisper, "So, come on: What's your thing?"

Is it obsessive punctuality? Is it always being late? Is it needing control over everyone and everything? Is it being impossibly breezy and carefree? Is it your constant one-upmanship in conversation? ("You went to Naples, Florida? Oh, I went to Naples, *Italy.*")

Is it your love of a good debate, of being the devil's advocate?

Is it your propensity to elevate other people's needs above your own?

Is it your utter disdain for all technology?

Is it your laughing at inappropriate times?

Is it your weddedness to sarcasm?

Is it your inability to take a joke?

Is it that weird, condescending tone you get whenever you think you're right?

No, really, now I'm asking! What would you say is your thing?

Just curious: Where do you think your thing came from? What experiences or inputs or assumptions have helped form that thing in your life?

Now, you know how Jess and I feel about the quirks that make you you. Don't go living to try to please all the people all the time, like your good pal Amy over here. You are amazing as-is—please believe me! And yet in the same breath, I will tell you that if there is something we can do to avoid future friendship hards, we might want to take a look at that.

> To be everything to everyone at all times? Whoosh. It makes you lose a little piece of yourself. It makes you push down who you really are and go silent about all the things you really want to say. It makes you forget the million little pieces that have gone into building you into the woman you're supposed to be. It's like handcuffing yourself to everyone else's opinion of what makes you worthy.

So, I think the question at hand is this one: How do we preserve the core of who we are while at the same time acknowledging that "who we are" has some issues, some quirks, some *challenges* to relational peace?

Ah. Let us begin!

I'm going to lay out the four things I always think about, whenever I come up against my thing. As you'll recall, my thing is having someone not like me, which feels daunting, a problem that can't be solved. I hate it. *Haaate* it. And yet does that keep it from happening to me? It does not. Not even once. So, I can either keep beating my head against so many walls in frustration, or I can behave like a grown adult.

If you, too, would like to behave like a grown adult, then read on. Adults only here, my friend.

The first thing about dealing with your things: Recognize—acknowledge—the thing. Seems obvious, right? It's not. Have you ever been talking to a friend and said in passing something like, "You know how you're always late? Well . . ." and then that friend totally freaks out? She sits up straighter and says, "What do you mean I'm always late?" and then things spiral downward from there?

So often, we don't know our own things until someone we trust points them out to us. If you didn't readily write down your thing earlier because you are just sure that you *have* no things, let me encourage you to get to a friend or family member quickly so that they can straighten things out for you.

We all have a thing.

Many of us—ahem—have *multiple* things.

The first thing about dealing with them rightly? *It's admitting what they are.*

Your turn: Write down—again—your thing. But this time, take your best shot at also logging the effects of your thing in your life. What does your thing cause you to assume? To say? To do? To believe? Get down as many nuances here as you can.

* * *

Ready for the second thing? It's this: *Work with the good that's there.*

In the same way that every cloud has a silver lining (I guess that's true, anyway), every "thing" has a beautiful upside, something that counterbalances its negative form. For example, one of the lovely byproducts of being a world-class people pleaser is that I'm generally the first person in a given situation to factor in everyone's needs and desires. I can be very compassionate. I can spot a marginalized person a mile away. I am truly a phenomenal listener. I genuinely care what you think.

Your turn: What is the upside to your less-than-great thing? What benefits do you see?

* * *

The third thing about dealing with your things is to *keep from being overtaken by the bad that's also there.*

Our things are our things because they kind of drag us down. No sense denying it, right? When we say we "have a thing," we're not bragging; we're confessing. So, yes, there are negatives associated with our things. There are challenges there we must face. But that doesn't mean we should be overtaken. We don't need to let our things win the day.

Your turn: How will you stop your freefall whenever you're at risk of being overrun by your thing? What encouragement from a friend, Scripture passages, positive self-talk, or key reminder will you bring to mind to keep you from being taken down?

> Run with arms wide open toward faith and hope. Give grace. Chase after gratitude. Bring joy with you everywhere you go. Do what God's asked you to do and keep your eyes on him. Be encouraging and kind and open. Keep fighting whatever your thing is. You might not wake up and instantly be cured, but take little steps every single day to get closer to where you want to be and then breathe. A pure heart won't be enough for everyone, but it'll be enough in the end.

You've told me what you'd do, so now it's my turn. Check the sidebar above for my full response. Anything in there feel helpful to you, too? I would be so *pleased* if you borrowed my thoughts.

WHAT NOW?

As something of a closing exercise, I want to ask you to do something that on the surface might seem a little weird. (Promise me you'll still like me when we're done?) Here goes: I want you to read the next paragraph and then copy it word for word on the lines on the next page. No skimping or corner-cutting, deal? I'm talking verbatim: *Word for word*. Once you're done, answer the final question of the lesson. Extra points for acting on the answer you provide.

Now, to that paragraph:

The right people will accept me because I am myself, not in spite of it. The right people will love me because of my passions, my ideas, and my opinions, not in spite of them. The right people will never mind being told no every once in a while because they will genuinely want me to be happy. The right people will yearn to know me in a substantial and meaningful way. True: Not everyone will be for me. But the right ones absolutely will be. And the right ones are the only ones I need.

Last question: Who are some of the "right people" you've known along the way? Consider thanking God for them. Consider thanking them directly, too.

7

When Fake Makes You Want to Hurl

Friendship should feel like coming home, not like tiptoeing around in a glass castle.

Based on Chapter 7

Jess

GET GOING

Can I ask you a question? How real are you? I mean in friendship, in any relationship, really, what percentage of the time do you spend posing and primping and presenting some idealized version of yourself, and what percentage of the time do you let the real you out?

No judgment here—honest. It can take a *lifetime* to move past the cultural pressure to perform, the messaging we pick up along the way that our value is somehow tied to our image, and our own perfectionistic fantasies. And yet if I were shooting straight I'd tell you that *you haven't really lived until you've really been yourself with those you love.*

In chapter 7 of the book, I said (and absolutely meant) this: "*Friendship should be the place that we walk into with our bare feet and our favorite sweatpants. It should be the place where we lay it all out and nothing stays hidden. It should be the place where we come as we are and we snuggle up on the corner of the couch and share our dreams, our fears, our joys, and our struggles. It should be the place where we're known and loved and given the benefit of the doubt. It should be the place where we are safe to just be. It should be the place where we can eat thousands of calories worth of brownies and ice cream. It should be the place where we can vent without being judged. It should be the place where we can ugly cry and snort laugh. It should be the place where we feel absolute belonging.*"

If you were to riff on what friendship should be, what things would make your list?

Friendship should be the place where . . .

- ______
- ______
- ______
- ______
- ______
- ______
- ______
- ______
- ______
- ______

CATCH YOUR BREATH

Such an idyllic vision we can paint for friendship, right? Nothing wrong with that. Sit with that dream-state you've written up before rushing to see what's next. How does your version of friendship make you feel? What emotions are present right now?

DIVE DEEP

In our heart of hearts, we know what's possible, where friendship is concerned. We've seen it and tasted it from time to time, so we know for sure that it's out there. If we could just find it a little more often, right? If that magical state could be just a *bit* more predictable to us.

But that's usually not the case. What we almost always find on the friendship front is a poor approximation of what it *should be*. Cattiness in high school bathrooms, anyone? Being marginalized because you bought the wrong jeans? Finding out you're the subject of gossip? Being judged harshly for standing your ground? Having your friend group leave you off the invitation list? Being overlooked for a job you wanted because a friend wouldn't serve as a reference for you?

Dig back through your own memory bank for two or three times when your vision for what friendship *could be* and the realities of what friendship *had become for you* were not at all aligned. What were the circumstances involved in each situation? How does each memory sit in your heart?

1.

2.

3.

These gaps in what we hope for in our friendships and what we're actually experiencing day by day can feel impossible to bridge, can't they? It's agonizing to hold out hope for a reality that feels elusive—slippery—at best.

Can I tell you something? I'm sorry. Truly. I'm sorry for the pain you've known.

I'm sorry for the pain I've known as well. *It just shouldn't be this hard.* And yet here is what I want to remind us both, now that we're staring at the pain of our past: *Yesterday's pain can help us be a better friend today, if we'll let it.* Let's look at how that works.

For starters, how would you put into three or four words the pain you've experienced when friendship didn't go as planned? Would you describe that pain as the pain of being "ostracized" or the pain of "feeling left out"? Or maybe it was the pain that "gossip" brings or the pain caused by a friend's "deceit." Fill each of the boxes below with a single word or phrase.

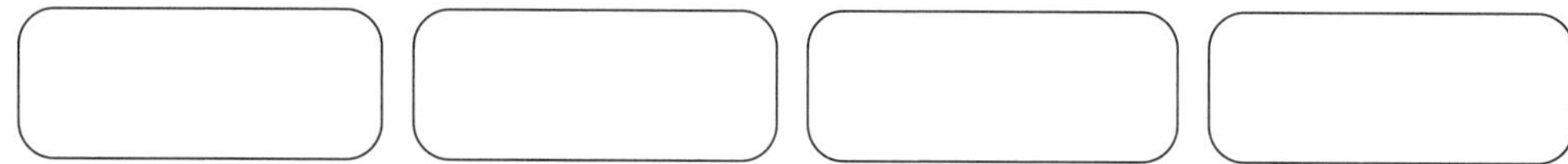

Next, think about how you'd answer this question: How might the pain you've experienced in past friendships help you make today's friendships better somehow? What can you offer to someone that you yourself never received?

The crazy reality is this: Sometimes the most compassionate people are the ones who have been denied compassion. Sometimes the most generous people are the ones who have been denied generosity. Sometimes the most gracious people are the ones who have been denied grace. My point: Whatever you were denied during those painful seasons is likely the exact thing God longs to use to impact your corner of the world. I remain convinced that all the annoyingly fluffy, superficial exchanges I had along the way make me the no-frills, no-sheen defacto poster child for depth and authenticity I am today.

Your pain becomes your offering to a friend who is struggling like you struggled back then. It's your credentials to be able to say, "I get it. I've been there, too."

> Is there anything better than opening up and being met with gracious understanding? Is there anything better than being met with a "me, too," or an "I've been there" or an "I'm here"? Is there anything better than getting all those pent-up feelings out on the table and being loved and accepted for who you are and where you are? Is there anything better than being truly known without secrets? Is there anything better than not being lonely in your struggle anymore? I don't know if there is.

WHAT NOW?

Friendship can be painful, but that pain doesn't have to keep us at home, alone. Before you zip to the next lesson, think of a few ways you might convert the awkwardness and ickiness you've dealt with before to something useful and productive today. If a painful friendship season included a friend who was really judgmental and harsh with you, then maybe you want to lead with unflappable encouragement, with affirming words, with a little dose of TLC.

If part of your pain journey included friends who chronically forgot to include you, then you might pay special attention whenever you get that feeling while making plans with friends that someone may feel left out.

If part of your pain involved having a friend who said yes easily but then typically bailed at the last minute, then perhaps you'll elevate the quality of follow-through. Maybe you'll be a "yes is yes" kind of friend.

Some ideas for how I'll convert my past pain into present value-adds . . .

-
-
-
-
-
-
-
-
-
-

8

When You're Stuck on the Outside

Before God gives you the microphone, he's going to make you walk the mountain. Before you find success, he's going to let you struggle. Before you get the gold, he's going to let you dig your way through a good bit of garbage.

Based on Chapter 8

Amy

GET GOING

I want to stick with the theme Jess introduced in the last lesson—that the greatest hurts we suffer personally can become our areas of greatest helpfulness relationally—by drilling down into one hurt in particular: *Finding yourself on the lonely outside of an inside circle of friends.*

You and I both have been there. *Everyone* has been there. Not a single woman I know has been exempt from at one time or another feeling horribly and totally left out. (Even Lysa TerKeurst, as I mentioned in the book. And who would leave *Lysa* out?)

> Circles can be awfully cruel. They can be cliquish and childish. They can be excluding and oh-my-gosh exhausting.

What was the situation for you? Describe a time when you felt horribly and totally left out.

CATCH YOUR BREATH

This might feel weird for you, but I want to invite you to pray a prayer of thanksgiving for that awful being-left-out episode. Not kidding. By the end of this lesson, you'll understand why, but for now, as much as you are able, get your heart and your mouth to say "thanks."

"Thank you, God, for the awfulness.

"And thank you for the good I'm trusting will come from it."

DIVE DEEP

I know that when you're feeling lonely, it seems like you're the only person on the planet who has ever been lonely before. Trust me: As we looked at in a previous lesson, it just ain't the case. If you still don't believe me, ask around. "Have you ever felt lonely?" you might ask someone, to which *to a person* they will say yes. Some studies show that one in three people feel not just anecdotally lonely but rather *chronically* lonely—lonely all the time. And the rates of loneliness are increasing so much these days that it is officially being called an epidemic.

Not good, right?

Here's the silver lining on that admittedly very dark cloud: If you have experienced loneliness before, and if so many people are either sometimes or all-the-time lonely today, then you have quite a gift to offer to the people you come across in daily life.

> The people who make the best friends are usually the ones who need a best friend.

Before we go on, talk to me. How do you see loneliness affecting your corner of the world these days? What effect is social media having on this dynamic, in your view?

Just after my husband, our newborn, and I moved to the town we now call home, I fell into a pretty deep pit of loneliness. It was bad. It was hard. It was a season I don't care to repeat. It felt to me like the entire rest of the world was inside of a circle that I was standing on the outside of. I hated that feeling! I desperately wanted a friend.

The wildest part about that period of my life is that I would have made a fantastic friend. I had very few obligations, so I had time to invest. I spent all day every day with a colicky baby, so I had conversational energy to spare. And I was brand new to town, so I had zero preferences on where to go and what to do. I'd have gone anywhere and done anything just to have something on the calendar that didn't involve nursing, diapers, or puke.

And yet, there I sat in my bubble of isolation, day after day after day.

Torment, I'm telling you. And yet I'm guessing you can relate.

When have you walked through an extended season of isolation, either because you chose it or because it somehow (cruelly!) chose you?

While I hope never to endure that kind of loneliness again, I thank God for it today. Why, you ask? Why would I do such a crazy thing? Because while I don't necessarily *enjoy* this reality, I accept that *growth only comes through pain*.

Let me pause here a moment and ask you to reflect on the most significant seasons of growth you've known. Maybe you were the first person to go to college in your family, and that experience required some serious growth.

Maybe you took a job you weren't *quite* qualified for and had to grow, grow, grow right from the start. Maybe you entered a meaningful relationship before you fully understood just what the other person would require of you, and it was straight-on grow or go. Maybe you became a mama for the first time. Hello! Growth, anyone?

Tell me about a few of your seasons of significant growth. What were the circumstances involved, and what was required of you in each?

1.

2.

3.

Now, looking back on each of those seasons of growth, what kind of pain did you have to endure? Was it the pain of having to learn new communication skills to be able to relate to someone you cared deeply about? Was it the pain of needing better time-management strategies so that you could finally succeed at work? Was it the pain of learning to let go of self-loathing so that you could thrive in a whole new way? In the space below, note what it looked like for you.

So, while that season of loneliness for me was wildly painful, it was also true that I *grew.* I learned some things. I developed some skills. I carved out greater capacity for courage to show up in my life. And now, what I'd like to do is invite you into that growth. First, we'll address the problems. Second, we'll come up with a plan.

If you are enduring a spurt of loneliness right now, please, please take heart. There is a way out of that dark, scary forest, and that path is already paved. Better still, once you muster the courage to put one foot in front of another, you can help someone learn to do the same.

* * *

Problem #1: *We Don't Stand on Common Ground*

On countless occasions, you and I both encounter women just like us throughout the course of our daily lives. Across the park, we see a mama sitting on a bench who has a son the same age as our son. While waiting in line at the print shop at Staples, we overhear a woman talking to the clerk about the signage she needs for her small business and think, "Hey, I own my own business, too." At the grocery store, we grin as we spot the woman in front of us unloading onto the conveyor belt thingy six cases of Diet Coke. Who knew we weren't the only ones who drank soda at that impressive pace?

We see these people and are drawn to these people, and yet guess what we choose to do?

Nothing. *Nothing*—that's what we do. Sure, we might smile a little half-smile, the kind of smile that invites nothing and gets nothing as a result. But we don't open our countenance. We don't speak. We don't reach out. We don't *engage.*

> Once you muster the courage to put one foot in front of another, you can help someone learn to do the same.

Question for you: If you can relate to these scenarios, then why haven't you engaged?

Let's keep going, and then we'll form an action plan. Hint: You're about to be asked to engage!

Problem #2: *We Too Easily Dismiss the Friends of Friends*

Here's the next problem: We meet the friends of our current friends and neglect to create a meaningful memory with them. Think: The book-loving mama you (also a book lover) meet at your friend's kid's birthday party. The single mama you meet at a friend's cookout who has the very same struggles as you. The foodie you meet at your friend's after-work happy hour who knows and loves *all* the dives you haunt. Your friend's neighbor who pops over while you're at your friend's house who just started attending the church where you go.

Ever had this happen? Think back. When have you met (and were drawn to) a friend of your friend but neglected to then follow up? Describe the situation and the reason you felt kinship with her. What kept you from reaching out later on? What kept the relationship stalled at one isolated event?

1.

2.

3.

Problem #3: *We Leave Outsiders on the Outside*

Ready for problem 3? It's this: We see an outsider at some gathering, someone who is clearly not included in whatever social thing is going on. We have been there! We know the feeling! We know how terrible that feeling feels! And yet again, we choose to do nothing. We do nothing to draw her in.

What assumptions, insecurities, or other reservations tend to keep you from drawing an outsider in? Anything below ring true for you? What would you add to the list?

- ○ "I don't want to bug them."
- ○ "Just don't have time."
- ○ "I'm an introvert. No, thanks."
- ○ "Too much potential drama there."
- ○ "What if they think I'm a freak?"
- ○ "Maybe they're there on purpose."
- ○ "I have enough problems of my own."
- ○ "________________________."
- ○ "________________________."
- ○ "________________________."
- ○ "________________________."

All right. Enough talk about the problems. Let's start solutioning now.

WHAT NOW?

Now, to the plan . . .

I'm sure you know what's coming next, which is my invitation to you and me both to start *doing* the very things we've been *avoiding*—and in so doing, welcoming lonely people in. Want to know how it works? It's easier than you may think. In fact, if you only remember one thing from this entire lesson, I hope it's this singular prompt: *Ask a question.*

To stand on common ground once you discover it, simply *ask a question.*

To engage with friends of friends, simply *ask a question.*

To invite outsiders in, simply *ask a question.*

Seriously? That's it? That's what we've been building to all this time?

Yep. Yep. And a third time, for good measure: Yep.

Smiling is good. Giving a quick head nod of acknowledgment is good. Making a passing comment—"Love your bag!"—is also good. But none of those things moves a fledgling relationship forward. None of those things squelches loneliness. None of those things forges a connection between you and them.

And so, the question. When it doubt, *question* it out.

* * *

Expert question-askers report that an easy thing to remember when wading into conversation with someone new is simply to start with a question that can be answered either with a number or a yes/no. For example:

1. "Does your family live near this park?"
2. "How long have you lived here?"
3. "Are you loving this warmer weather?"

Easy, right? A number, or a yes/no.

Then, after you ask and hear the answer to *that* question, you can move to something that invites a little dialogue. For example, sticking with our three scenarios above, you might ask:

- "Oh, you live right there! Good deal. What else do you and your kids like doing together besides coming to the park?"

- "Five weeks! Welcome to town. What motivated you to move here five weeks ago?"
- "Ah, a winter-weather lover! Well, from your perspective, what makes winter better than all the other seasons?"

From there, just see what unfolds. Maybe nothing will unfold. *But maybe something will.* Maybe that park mama will say, "You know, we are here literally every afternoon at one. Would love to see you here and let the kids play awhile."

Maybe that recent transplant to your town will ask something like, "You don't know of any pet-sitters around here, do you?" to which you might say, "Actually, my eleven-year-old daughter just started a pet-sitting business. I'd be happy to introduce you to her."

Maybe that snow-loving friend of a friend will say, "If you ever want to try snowshoeing, I've got an extra pair."

Who knows where it will go, or if it will go at all. The point isn't the result of the effort. The point is the effort itself.

Want to give it a try? What are a few opening questions and a few deeper questions you might ask a perfect stranger, in hopes of drawing her in? Granted, the "deeper" questions are sometimes easier to come up with once you have an answer to the opening ones. But just play with the ideas for now. Imagine a few scenarios involving places you frequent these days—the grocery store, your kid's soccer game, the gym, your neighborhood streets—and see what you come up with. No right or wrong answers—well, *questions*—here.

Opening Questions I Could Ask:

1.

2.

3.

4.

5.

> Build your own space and look around and gather up all the women you notice hanging outside of that tight radius. You will find some of your best friends there, friends who have room for friendship . . . friends who will make room for you.

As you go about your daily life, friend, never forget how it felt to be excluded, to be on the outside looking in. You know that fresh agony. You wouldn't wish it on anyone, right? So, instead of furthering another person's pain today, seek to lift it, to relieve it a bit. Reach out. Put a smile on your face. Ask a question—and the next question after that. Be the person you have prayed for, each time you've been left out. Let your cuts help another to heal.

9

When You Cram All Your Junk in the Closet and Slam the Door

Invite people into your life as is. Your face as is, your heart as is, your thighs as is.

Based on Chapter 9

Jess

GET GOING

Smart people who know a lot about advertising say that even for the biggest-name brands out there, what they peddle to us unsuspecting consumers isn't their latest gadget or gizmo or goose-down comforter. But rather a lifestyle that has *energy* to learn the gadget or *time* to play with the gizmo or *enough leisurely mornings* to be

found lounging underneath a comforter instead of racing around like a crazed, headless chicken, begging everyone to *load up, already.* They know that we don't need a new comforter. They know that what we need is a vacation. A massage. Yes, a morning to stay in bed. (And not because we're sick. Sick mornings do not count as rest.)

What they've tapped into is the fact that because we are so desperate for a break, we will buy absolutely *anything* if it is set in the context of a break. The fourteen-dollar deodorant is worn by the guy whose muscles are absolutely popping through his shirt, even though what he appears to be doing now is giving his Boston terrier a belly rub while lounging in sweatpants and socks.

So, the four-hundred-dollar sweater is worn by the twiggy girl enjoying a carefree stroll across the Scottish Highlands. The forty-thousand-dollar minivan is driven by a mom who despite her evidently needing seating for eight in her everyday vehicle has perfectly styled loose curls, professionally manicured fingernails, and *makeup* on.

I'm telling you: We're suckers for this stuff every time. If only our house could be as tidy as houses are on TV! If only our cars were as pristine as cars are on Internet ads! If only our closets were as meticulously organized as closets look on the Home Edit's Instagram feed!

If only, right?

If only.

What real life is like instead? Puffiness and wrinkly-ness that *no* amount of makeup can cover. A living room so carpeted in Legos that it is literally impossible to traverse its expanse. And yes, as I confessed in the book, a fully intact, wrapped McDonald's cheeseburger pulled from my giant purse by my friend the other day, which had been in there for who knows how long. She was looking for lip balm. She got a reminder instead: "I'm gross," I said without one ounce of shame. "Just deal."

Your turn. Are you the type who pours store-bought salad dressing into a quaint, farm-style serving jar before guests arrive? Like me, are you the type who crams everything into an out-of-the-way closet when a friend is dropping by so that she will (falsely) believe that you're neat? Are you the type who speed-cleans the inside of your vehicle before swinging by to give a pal a ride so that she isn't horrified by the stench?

What are you known to do in secret, so that people think well of you? (I would give anything to know what you're about to say. If we ever meet in person, do tell!)

1.

2.

3.

4.

5.

> I'm the hostess who hides her mess in the coat closet and slams the door before it all avalanches its way onto the floor. I'm the hostess who never has enough forks. It's cool if I eat with my hands bear-style, right? I'm the hostess who once forgot to include the correct ingredients for boxed brownies and nearly made my guest lose a crown on her back tooth.

CATCH YOUR BREATH

I make light of our tendency to hide the real-deal us with friends, but of course there's a serious side to this discussion too. Before moving into the heart of this lesson, take a minute or two and ask yourself, "Why *do* I feel the need to hide what's real, what's true, what's me?"

DIVE DEEP

As I wrote in the corresponding chapter to this lesson, it's completely natural for us to want people to think highly of us. Nobody wants to be known as a hoarder, a slacker, a slob. So of course I'm not suggesting that you ban cleaning your home ever again, all for the sake of authenticity. What I am saying is that if you're struggling to establish and maintain close friendships, it could be that a little transparency is in order for you.

What might you say or do if you were a little more transparent in your friendships? What has kept you from saying and doing those things thus far?

Let me ask you an honest question: Of the people in your life you consider close friends, what do you value in them?

Think of the friendships you think most highly of today. What characteristics do you appreciate most in those friends?

Out of curiosity, did "impressive" make the list? What about "cleanliness"? Oh, how about, "her ability to make homemade salad dressing"? My guess is that while your friend's homemade salad dressing may in fact be your favorite salad dressing in the world, her ability to make it was found exactly nowhere on your list.

I'm going to say something that very well may blow your mind. You ready? Here goes: Your mess doesn't make you unfriendable. In fact, if you invite people into your mess, you're creating space for them to have their mess, too.

Test out my theory, if you will. Describe a time when you have allowed a friend into your mess—a messy house, a messy car, a messy marriage, a messy heart—and you didn't die.

Now the same idea, in reverse: When did you enter a friend's mess—either by her invitation or by accident when you just dropped by—and the world kept on spinning then, too?

See? You've done both. You've survived both. And I bet you collected great stories to tell. (You do, right? Well, let's hear one.)

What meaningful memory or hilarious adventure did you rack up one time, because either you or a friend decided to get real?

You see, there are really only two ways to deal with the inevitable messes we make every day: We can either hide the mess, or we can herald it . . . we can either showcase it or stuff it away. But believe me when I tell you, only one of those ways helps friendships deepen; only one helps friendships to grow.

Let me ask you: What mess are you forever mopping up these days? What's got you shaking your head while you mutter curse words? What's got you wringing your hands in frustration and angst? Clearly we're not talking about Cheerios on the floorboard here, but rather a gut-level, soul-level *mess*. What's yours, and where did it come from? How is it affecting your day-to-day world?

Now to the friendship side of the equation: Who gets to see the mess? I mean it: Who will you let into that mess—not necessarily to help clean it up, but to shake her fist at life's audacity, too?

The truth of the matter is that it's tough to embrace a façade. Yeah, you can order your world in such a way that people around you really do believe that you have it all together on a 24/7 basis. But honestly: *Where's the fun in that?* Intimacy is gained in the endless cycle of you letting your friend in, which prompts her to then let you in, which prompts you to let her in again, which prompts her to let you in. On and on it goes until you wake up a decade later and ask, "How did we even meet?"

> Friendship is not a stage on which you have to perform, and it isn't a popularity contest. True friendship is where messes belong.

WHAT NOW?

I'm not sure what adding a little more transparency and vulnerability will mean for you today. Maybe it's showing up to a lunch date without makeup on for once. Maybe it's saying, "Of course we can have book club here" when the other hostess cancels at the last minute and then refusing to stress over your cluttered living room and unswept floors. Maybe it's giving an honest answer when a friend texts, "Hey, you doing okay?"

Something's probably percolating in that beautiful brain of yours. What can you do this week to peel back the façade a little and risk letting a friend see you for real?

When It All Feels Like High School 2.0

Don't push other women out. Hold them close. Don't look at them as competition. Look at them as inspiration.

Based on Chapter 10

Amy

GET GOING

You and I both recognize that we're no longer in high school anymore. For starters, there's the fact that we buy our own groceries now. And maybe pay rent or a mortgage. And perhaps have miniature humans relying on us for, oh, things like *everything*. So, if we're so clearly not in high school now, then why do messages we picked up way back then haunt us still today?

What messages did you pick up in your teenage years that whisper to you still?

"Psst . . . you're . . .

CATCH YOUR BREATH

Take a moment to sit with those messages, the ones you've now written out in your own handwriting. Does seeing them on the page like this cause you to view them differently than ever before?

DIVE DEEP

Try though we might, sometimes these whispers turn into shouts that demand to be heard. How annoying it is, when we finally realize that we've been being governed by our fifteen-year-old selves!

The impact of this dynamic is anything but benign. In my experience, listening to these messages is just the first step down the spiral of despair. We listen to the messages. We believe the messages. We buy into the drama of the whole deal. And we find ourselves totally derailed.

There must be a better way.

There is, in fact, a better way.

If you're tired of letting your thoughts—and, by definition, your life—be led by errant messages that were handed to you years or decades ago, then stick around. That spiral? It goes both ways.

> In high school, there's such a high priority on getting ahead of everyone else. So much of girls' time is spent obsessed with being the girl who has the most—the most friends, the most boyfriends, the most awards, the most A's, the most extracurricular activities, the most clothes, the most parties to attend—but the only thing this does is cause competition, comparison, jealousy, self-doubt, impersonating, posing, pretending, pushing people down to get ahead, and drama. So much stinking drama.

Take a look at the sidebar regarding what you and I both probably focused on way too much in high school. How do those trends manifest themselves today in your life? Sure, maybe you're not trying to get better grades than other girls anymore, but are you now pitting your kids' grades against those of your friends' kids? Note a few ways each of the ol' high-school dynamics show up for you here and now.

Competition

Comparison

> It's time we stop trying to steal each others' crowns. It's time we stop clawing at each other and climbing over each other to get ahold of something that was never meant for us. Her crown isn't going to fit you. It's not going to look good on you. Let her have it and relax. What's meant for you will come for you.

Jealousy

Self-doubt

Impersonating/pretending to be someone you're not

Posing

Pretending

Pushing people down to get ahead

Drama

* * *

One of the most wonderful parts of being an adult is getting to *choose who you will be*. When you're a child, things are decided for you—what you'll wear, when you'll eat, where you'll go, what you'll do. But as an adult—just think of it!—the person now choosing is *you*. What this means is that if you don't want to play the comparison game any longer, *you don't have to play*. If you don't want to be ruled by jealousy, *you don't have to be ruled by that.* If you don't want to pretend to be someone you're not, *you absolutely don't have to pretend.*

Now, I'm not suggesting that the actions required to live the life we long for are easy to take. I'm just saying they're take-able. (Welcome to "Make Up New Words with Amy." Glad you're here.)

Without stressing about how in the world you're going to muster the courage, creativity, strength, and stamina to actually implement the following statements, give me a few of the "I don't have to's" now rattling around in your mind, truths that someday might just lead you to becoming the person you long to be. "I don't have to be petty!" "I don't have to denigrate myself!" "I don't have to wear the scratchy wool sweater of anxiety all the stinkin' time!" Now, you try:

I don't have to

I don't have to

I don't have to

I don't have to

I don't have to

I don't have to

I don't have to

I don't have to

> We can choose to live in freedom. God isn't handing out cool points, and he definitely hasn't pitted us against one another.

You see, when you realize that you have *agency* in this whole situation, you prove to yourself and to the world that you're not in high school anymore. Am I right? What drives a high schooler? Mom and Dad's opinions, for starters. Next up? Hormones! Emotions! Drama on steroids at all times. We've progressed beyond on all that, yes? We've *grown*. We've *matured*. We've learned neat tricks like *self-control*.

Sister, we can pick who we are. We can pick who we're not. We can pick how we'll show up in the world.

Now, in case you need a little tune-up for your picker, I'm going to loan you the perfect thing: *Truth*. Did you know that God thinks you're cool? He does. He totally does. And did you know that once you truly believe that God thinks you're cool, you tend to hold yourself higher just a bit? And did you know that when you are feeling more confident and self-assured in the world, you fall prey to drama less often than before?

It's true. It's *all* true. And it can all be traced back to truth.

Take a look at the Bible verses on the next page—I've stuck them all right there in the chart for you. In the space beside each one, I want you to write out the verse or verses in the first person. Meaning, if the verse says, "God so loved the world that . . . ," I want you to turn that into, "God so loved me that . . ." Make sense? All right. See you on the other side.

THE TRUTH ABOUT ME

ORIGINAL VERSES	PERSONALIZED FOR ME
"For God so loved the world that he gave his one and only Son, that whoever believes in him shall not perish but have eternal life." (John 3:16)	
"How priceless is your unfailing love, O God! People take refuge in the shadow of your wings." (Psalm 36:7)	
"Be strong and courageous. Do not be afraid; do not be discouraged, for the LORD your God will be with you wherever you go." (Joshua 1:9)	
"The LORD your God is with you, the Mighty Warrior who saves. He will take great delight in you; in his love he will no longer rebuke you, but will rejoice over you with singing." (Zephaniah 3:17)	

What do you think would unfold in your thought life, in your heart, and in your friendships if you were to fixate on messages such as these, instead of the messages you picked up as a kid?

WHAT NOW?

The life you're wishing for? It's sitting there, waiting to be lived. It's waiting for you to live it—do you see? The choice, as always, is yours. And what I have seen with my own two eyes to be true is that as soon as you decide to rise above the lies you used to believe, you help each of your friends rise, too.

> When we get our minds right, and we get into a secure, mature rhythm, the people around us rise right along with us—and that is the goal. That's the whole point of it all, the entire meaning of friendship: That we do it in a way that lifts everyone in the group.

Which brings me to this idea: What if this week you were to intentionally and authentically reach out to a friend with a word of encouragement and celebration?

Think of someone who has met a goal, reached a milestone, achieved an award . . . maybe just made it through the week in one piece . . . and commit to celebrating the accomplishment with her. You might say something such as:

- "I celebrate this news with you!"
- "What a win! How do you feel?"
- "You must feel *amazing*. Tell me all about it . . ."
- "You should feel *so* proud of yourself. Do you?"

Who's it going to be? What accomplishment did she bag? What do you think you'll say?

When You're a Bad Friend

Let's normalize the fact that sometimes we're the problem. Let's normalize the fact that we're a bunch of imperfect people learning and just doing our best.

Based on Chapter 11

Jess

GET GOING

You're probably seeing a theme with these lessons so far, which is that *there is just so much that you and I can do* to become more aware, to sharpen our skills, to deepen our understanding of what makes friendships work, and more. We can get better. We can become wiser. We can grow stronger. We can *improve*—we really can.

And yet.

(This is where I burst the bubble. You gathered that, yes?)

And yet, improve as we do, we won't get it right every time.

When have you clearly "gotten it wrong" in friendship? What was the situation, and what do you so wish you hadn't done?

CATCH YOUR BREATH

Take a moment to receive the fact that we *all* goof from time to time. You're in good company here! This lesson isn't intended to shame you. Its goal is to help you move forward in integrity after the regrettable thing has been done.

DIVE DEEP

If you're like 99.9 percent of the population, then the number of times when you have gotten it wrong in friendship is too many times to count. Friendship is tough! Close friendships? Even tougher. So many moving pieces. So many emotions to take into consideration. So many opportunities for things to go awry.

> Friendship is messy, and sometimes we're total jerkwads.

Take a look at the litany of ways we can get it wrong in friendship, and see what memories come to mind. Jot down any that pop to the surface for you . . . who was involved,

what happened in the moment, and what happened later as a result?

I was tired, so I . . .

I was distracted, so I . . .

I was thinking about a personal problem, so I . . .

I was just in a weird place, so I . . .

I was being ridiculous, so I . . .

I was feeling insecure, so I . . .

I was hurt, so I . . .

I was fearful, so I . . .

I felt left out, so I . . .

I felt neglected, so I . . .

I was sad, so I . . .

I was having trouble at home, so I . . .

I was PMS-ing, so I . . .

I needed attention, so I . . .

I was overwhelmed with life, so I . . .

Anything I missed here? If so:

I was .... *, so I . . .*

* * *

See what I mean? So many things play into our interactions with friends that it's no wonder we fumble here and there. As we've seen plainly here, the question isn't *if* we'll mess up, but rather how we'll recover *when* we do.

How easy is it for you to admit that you get it wrong in friendship from time to time?

- ◯ No problem here. Who doesn't?
- ◯ Honestly, most of the friendship rifts I've endured were not at all my fault.

To mature in our friendship quotient—our FQ, if you will—we need two things to be true:

1. We need to be clear on our limitations.
2. We need to be committed to our convictions.

If you think about it, disappointment in friendship simply cannot happen unless someone had an expectation that somehow went unmet. Maybe we knew nothing about the expectation, so violating it was an accident through and through. This would be called *lack of awareness*. Or maybe we *did* know about the expectation and violated it anyway. This would be called *lack of care*. Either way, when we get it wrong in friendship, we can be sure that at some point we violated a friend's expectation—overt, covert, either way.

When we follow those two handy guidelines above, these violations happen far less frequently because both you and your friend are clear on what you both can and cannot do.

Let me give you an example, and then I'll flesh out those guidelines with you.

Let's say you're the type of person who loves it when friends drop by without texting you in advance. You love the surprise factor. You appreciate the interruption—most likely because whatever that friend brings to bear on the situation is better than how the situation previously was. You love the camaraderie. The whole thing is just plain *great.*

Now, let's say that you establish a friendship with someone, and after many months of hanging out and grocery shopping together and helping each other plan your kids' birthday parties and more, you happen to be near her house one day while on your way home from a lunch meeting.

You know where this is going, don't you.

As soon as you realize where you are, you're elated. You'll pop in and say hey to your friend! How cool is this day, that you happen to be *right here*?

Flash forward to later that night. You're getting ready for bed and feel gross. Your friend was not what we would call *excited* to see you standing on her front porch, unannounced. Her living room was a wreck, her kitchen smelled weird, she hadn't had time to shower yet, and she needed to get her kids out the door to their piano lesson.

How could you not know that this would upset her? How had the two of you made it this far in your relationship without your having this crucial knowledge?

And yet this happens all. the. time. We think we know someone, and then *kaboom*, a bomb goes off. Worse yet, we were unwittingly the ones who set it off. Who knew we could be so destructive and dumb?

Enter those lovely guidelines, above.

Let's begin.

Be Clear on Your Limitations

If you live in the United States of America, then it's likely you aren't very comfortable talking about your limitations—that is, if you'll even admit that you *have* limitations. In this country, we tend to believe we can have it all—and with same-day shipping, no less. But try to fit twenty-five hours of obligations into a twenty-four-hour day, and even you will wind up saying, "Huh. There's evidently a limitation there."

The first guideline for avoiding getting it wrong in friendships as much as possible is to get clear on our limitations. Yes. Even you.

Do you have a spouse who travels twenty days a month? Do you have four kids under the age of ten? Do you barf every single time you eat cheese? Do you have insane work deadlines the third quarter of every year? Are you caring for aging parents? Do you live thirty-five minutes from the nearest Target? Are you incapable of finding jeans that fit your distinctive body type, regardless of how many stores you hit? Can you not sit still for more than twenty minutes, no matter how hard you try?

What limitations exist for you, in this specific season of life? Ready, set, get working on that you-centric list!

1. ______
2. ______
3. ______
4. ______
5. ______
6. ______
7. ______
8. ______
9. ______
10. ______

11. ______________________________
12. ______________________________
13. ______________________________
14. ______________________________
15. ______________________________
16. ______________________________
17. ______________________________
18. ______________________________
19. ______________________________
20. ______________________________
21. ______________________________
22. ______________________________
23. ______________________________
24. ______________________________
25. ______________________________

Be Committed to Your Convictions

Now, to guideline two. If limitations are the immovable boundaries surrounding your life, then convictions are the rules you prefer to play by while within those lines you've drawn. Are you more of a schedule-everything person or a free-form friend? Do you like to honor a full day of rest every week? Does your family sometimes enjoy a phone-free weekend? Would you rather receive a phone call or a text? Do you think Halloween is of the devil, or are you the host of the neighborhood's favorite haunted house every single year? Do you love yoga? Do you eat dessert before dinner, just in case?

Diet Coke or soda will kill you?

Sun worshiper or SPF 50?

Coffee or tea?

Dogs or cats? (Duh. No brainer. Sorry, cat friends.)

Makeup daily or no?

What delights you? What bugs you to no end? What is most important in life? What books simply *must* be read?

You get the idea. Convictions. Yours. Go.

What are some of the convictions you hold that totally make you you?

1. ______
2. ______
3. ______
4. ______
5. ______
6. ______
7. ______
8. ______
9. ______
10. ______
11. ______
12. ______

13. ____________________

14. ____________________

15. ____________________

16. ____________________

17. ____________________

18. ____________________

19. ____________________

20. ____________________

21. ____________________

22. ____________________

23. ____________________

24. ____________________

25. ____________________

WHAT NOW?

What to do, once you've made your lists? I have some ideas on that! First, consider asking your closest friends to make similar lists of their own and then getting together to share what you've logged. (Please invite me to every one of these meetings. I would give *anything* to be a fly on those walls.)

Tell your friends what your limitations are. You will be shocked by how many of your real-deal limitations even your closest pals were totally unaware of. We think people think about us far more than they do! The reality is that we're all running fast and furious these days and can barely keep up with ourselves. So: Tell them. Lovingly. But tell them.

Tell your friends what your convictions are. Same song as the paragraph before, second verse. "Really?" a close friend will say to you. "You hate vegetables??"

Also: Listen carefully as your friends share their lists. Ask questions as they work through their limitations and convictions. Ask follow-up questions after that. Let them know you're dialed into them. Let them know you care. And know this: You're not learning this information to *please* anyone. (Go back through Amy's lesson on the perils of people-pleasing, if you need a refresher course.) You're not learning the info to please your friends. You're learning it to honor them. Huge difference between the two.

Let me push pause here. How are you feeling about all of this? What opportunities for intimacy do you see in your friendships by working through these guidelines with them?

1. ______________________________

2. ______________________________

3. ______________________________

4. ______________________________

5. ______________________________

Admittedly, it's not like sharing these details on one occasion with your friends will lock them in their brains for all time. But it will at least put the expectations out there, so that when things get wonky between you—and they *will* get wonky, you know—you can gently but confidently come to them and say, "I hate that I missed you all weekend. Just reunited with my phone this morning, and I see that you reached out a few times. Everything okay? I'm here now. How can I help?"

And when you (knowingly or unknowingly) violate one of their expectations, they can do the same for you.

* * *

It's worth noting here that when you are the violator—is that too strong a word?—there are a few extra steps I encourage you to take, to be sure you own the oops.

Of the five steps below, when things get sideways in a friendship and you're to blame, which is often the toughest for you to take?

- ○ **Step #1: Stay.** Connect with, instead of canceling, your friend.
- ○ **Step #2: Head straight for the fire.** Find out what's going on before the whole house burns down.
- ○ **Step #3: Clean up your mess.** Own your mistake and then stick around to fix whatever you broke.
- ○ **Step #4: Be real about your own hurt feelings and forgive.** Admit that you're not invincible, and that even if you are the culprit for why things went wrong, your feelings, too, were hurt.
- ○ **Step #5: Shake it off.** Leave space for failure in friendship and be gentle with yourself when you fail.

Certainly there will be times when these steps are insufficient to heal whatever has been broken between you and your friend. Abuse or rampant manipulation comes to mind. As does chronic deceit. There may come a time when you have to part ways for good with a friend, in which case these steps just don't apply. But for the majority of situations we'll face in our friendships, they'll work outright wonders for us.

Is there a friend you need to "work the steps with" this week? If yes, who is it? What's been going on between you?

What are you hoping reconciliation will include, based on the piece(s) you plan to own? Confirm your commitment here.

12

When You've Been There, Done That, and Had Your Heart Break

Friendships break. Friendships rip, and they shift, and they lose their strength from time to time.

Based on Chapter 12

GET GOING

With all the effort we pour into friendship, it's no wonder we feel totally devastated when for one reason or another one comes to an end. We want to find good friendships, right? Truer still, we want the good ones to stay.

What's the toughest friendship breakup you've known?

CATCH YOUR BREATH

Take a moment to just sit—still, quiet, eyes closed, alone. Replay a few favorite memories from that beloved friendship. Thank God that friendship exists. Thank God that *he* exists, to help us pick up the pieces and move on.

DIVE DEEP

In my view there are always two phases to a friendship breakup: There's the breakup itself, in all its awful, unwelcomed glory; and then there's what we'll do as a result of that breakup. Will we shuffle our feet and sulk forever? It's an option, you know. Or will we try to somehow make sense of the thing and use those lessons learned to build a better friendship next time?

(I guess if there's a third option, it's that we'll sort out those lessons but still sulk and shuffle awhile. That's what I always pick, anyway.)

> There's no formula for fixing everything, and there's no cure to help curate the perfect friendship. Nobody has it all figured out, and even the most experty of experts sometimes gets it wrong. Still: Trying is always the way to go. Reflect. Learn. Grow. And you'll be better able to move ahead.

The lessons you have learned from your friendship breakup are certainly different from mine. But in case you've never carved out time to think through what your lessons are, I'm going to lay mine out here, one by one. Maybe reading through—and reacting to—the understanding I've gained will help you begin to put words to yours. In hopes of that outcome, at the end of this lesson I've given you room to log *yours* one by one.

I feel like I need to cue the saddest song of the year—T. Swift's "Breathe," anyone?—as I write this. Whoosh. *Have I mentioned that friendship is hard?*

Lesson Learned #1: *Breakups are hard. Give yourself permission to feel.*

A friendship breakup is a loss, and losses must be grieved. We either voluntarily grieve them, or else we stuff down the pain until it seeps out sideways when we least expect it. Trust me: Voluntary is better. It's better every time.

How does this lesson resonate with your assumptions and firsthand experiences? That's the question I'd like you to answer following each one.

Lesson Learned #2: *Do things out of love, not desperation.*

While it's good to be loving and generous, it's also good to know when a relationship needs some room, some space. If that time has come, then with self-respect still intact, go ahead and take a step back.

Lesson Learned #3: *Bitterness is never the answer.*

Anger is understandable when a breakup has occurred, but it's never wise to let that anger morph into bitterness. Refuse to let yourself indulge hatred, villainization, gossip, slander, or drama of any kind. (We graduated from high school, remember? We're not mean girls anymore.)

> Bitterness is not a good home, and there is no warmth in resentment.

Lesson Learned #4: *Forgiveness is pretty good for everyone.*

Forgiveness isn't only a gift you give to the other person; it's a gift you give to yourself. Forgive. Forgive early. Forgive fully. Forgive with no expectations from the other person at all. Release your friend, and you'll simultaneously give yourself wings to fly.

Lesson Learned #5: *Shaming and blaming won't help you grow.*

Ever heard the phrase, "It takes two to tango"? There are two sides to every story, and there are two parties to every breakup. Stick to focusing on the part you need to own. This is where growth is found.

Lesson Learned #6: *There are things to learn here—valuable things.*

Who knows what you'll learn by walking through the tough stuff of life? The key isn't what life will teach you as much as it is your choosing to remain teachable through it all.

Lesson Learned #7: *Hold your integrity tight.*

It's easy to believe that when a friendship dies, we die, too. This simply isn't the case. Hold fast to what is true about you and to what is true about your future in Christ. If you're still here and you're still breathing, you still have life to live.

Lesson Learned #8: *Don't bring your old crap into a new house.*

Saddling a new friendship with your old baggage is self-sabotage at its worst. As you establish new connections, keep those connections free of the static you leave behind. There is so much hope and promise and potential in brand-new friendships! Let those things be.

Lesson Learned #9: *Sometimes things come back around.*

One of the main reasons to hold onto wise practices when you're reeling from a friendship breakup is that sometimes time really does heal old wounds and that friendship will be restored. Be the person now that you want to look back on with satisfaction, knowing you walked well through the fire and pain.

Lesson Learned #10: *And sometimes they don't, but that's okay, too.*

It's true: Sometimes friendships don't come back around. But know that the ache you feel is proof that you cared . . . that you engaged, that you encouraged, that you loved.

> Some relationships were meant to remain a memory, pictures in an old scrapbook that you can look back and smile on from time to time.

Your turn. If you were asked to contribute to an anthology on the wisest beliefs a sister could hold or the wisest actions a sister could take on the heels of a friendship breakup, which ones would you want to include? (If you've got more than five, log more than five. Go 'til you can't go no more.)

1.

2.

3.

4.

5.

> Don't run yourself down, but do assess your own actions. When we own our faults, we not only take away their power but also make it less likely that we'll make the same mistake twice.

WHAT NOW?

In chapter 12 of the book, I mentioned that one of the best ways I've found to get closure on a friendship breakup that still feels like it's rocking your world is to grab a journal and write down your thoughts. Plenty of ink has been spilled on the benefits of journaling, so I won't belabor the point here. I would simply invite you to give it a try.

If your thoughts still feel spinny, if your eyes still feel weepy, if your heart still feels like it might just beat out of your chest, then quick, find a journal, a pen, and an hour. Pick a list from the ones I've found helpful or come up with a few of your own.

LISTS TO HELP HEAL A BROKEN HEART

THINGS I LOVED ABOUT MY FRIEND.	THINGS I DID WELL IN OUR FRIENDSHIP.	THINGS SHE DID WELL IN OUR FRIENDSHIP.
Things that could have been better about how we related.	Reasons I'm proud of how I handled myself.	Things I'll look for in my next friendship.
Ways I judged (and still judge?) my friend unfairly.	Reasons I'm having a hard time moving on.	Things I can learn from our relationship.
Things I've forgiven her for.	Things I haven't forgiven her for.	Things I've forgiven myself for.
Things I'm sorry for.	Blessings I pray for her.	Things I'm grateful to God for because of knowing this friend.

Thank goodness Jesus' arms are wide and his heart has room for us all. Thank goodness that even at my smallest, he was big enough to save a wretch, a mess, a little lost soul like mine. Thank goodness for that cross, and thank goodness for therapists, too.

When Your Mouth Gets Sticky and Words Get Hard

Deep friendship requires honesty; it requires humility—especially when you're wrong—and it requires heartfelt apologies.

Based on Chapter 13

Jess

GET GOING

While making all those lists Amy recommended is an absolutely necessary first step, it's also true that sometimes those lists will show you with blinding clarity that a conversation you should have had along the way is still waiting to be had. You and I both know that it's far easier to have conversations *in our head* with someone who has hurt us than to risk speaking words aloud.

I'm here to ask you to take the risk.

When have you put a mental conversation on repeat while neglecting to ever approach that friend in person? What fears or insecurities generally keep you from facing conflict head-on?

It's a whole lot easier to focus on other people's flaws than to deal with my own heart issues. It's a whole lot easier to talk smack about someone than to have a conversation with them to figure things out.

CATCH YOUR BREATH

Take a moment to sit with the words of a favorite verse of mine. It goes like this: "God wants us to grow up, to know the whole truth and tell it in love—like Christ in everything" (Ephesians 4:15 MSG). Knowing the truth and telling the truth are two very different things, it appears. What's more, *telling* the truth and telling the truth *in love* . . . well, two very different things yet again.

DIVE DEEP

Look back at the work you did in lesson 12. Any friendship situations rise to the surface for you that are begging for a conversation to be had?

Go ahead and note them here. We'll come back to these friendships in a moment.

1.

2.

3.

4.

5.

Before we get into those pressing conversations that may need to be had, let's rewind your life a bit. I want you to think back on times when you have risked speaking truth to a friend on the heels of an infraction of some sort. Something went sideways. You felt wronged. And you mustered the courage to say so to her.

> Deep friendship requires deep honesty.

Got a few of these scenarios in mind? Log them on the grid on the next page.

TIMES WHEN I SPOKE TRUTH

THE SITUATION	WHAT I SAID	HOW THINGS WENT FROM THERE

Overall, would you say that choosing to speak up about rather than stuff down what you were thinking or feeling helped you or harmed you more? Further, did it help or harm the friendship? Note your thoughts on the matter below.

Similarly, when has a friend risked speaking truth to you? Same story, flip side. See what memories come to mind.

TIMES WHEN SOMEONE SPOKE TRUTH TO ME

THE SITUATION	WHAT SHE SAID	HOW THINGS WENT FROM THERE

Overall, would you say that having your friend speak up about rather than stuff down what she was thinking or feeling helped you or harmed you more? Further, did it help or harm the friendship? Note your thoughts on *this* matter below.

In the Bible, there is an interesting phrase that says, "As iron sharpens iron, so one person sharpens another" (Proverbs 27:17).

With these recollections in mind of how you've been impacted by the speaking of truth, how would you say you've been sharpened in the process? How have you been "honed"?

Here's another one, for your consideration: "Wounds from a sincere friend are better than many kisses from an enemy" (Proverbs 27:6 NLT).

Have you found this sentiment to be true for you? If so, in what ways?

WHAT NOW?

Two things I want to ask you to consider, as you wrap up this study with Amy and me:

1. Please follow through on having those conversations that need to be had.
2. Please pray before you have them that you'll see *truth* as truth really is and that you'll use words that convey nothing but *love.*

> We have the choice to focus on the things we find annoying or the things we find admirable. We have the power to suppress, and we have the power to set free.

What are your thoughts, as you read those requests?

And while there are no magic words you can speak that will guarantee the outcome of your dreams, let me leave you with a few well-placed word choices, both to invite and to communicate truth.

Words you might use to invite truth:

- "Hey, are we okay?"
- "Can I ask what you meant when you said . . ."
- "Are you upset with me?"
- "Have I hurt you, friend?"
- "I'd love to know how you're feeling . . ."
- "What caused that reaction from you?"
- "Am I being a good friend to you?"
- "What do you need that you haven't been getting?"

Words you might use to convey truth:

- "Did I understand you correctly that . . ."
- "When you (said/did) this, I felt . . ."
- "I've been struggling with . . ."
- "Can we talk for a sec?"
- "When you ________________, I feel ________________ . . ."
- "I was a jerk today, and I'm sorry. Will you forgive me for . . ."
- "After I said that, I realized it was insensitive. I am so sorry for . . ."
- "You're right. I am so sorry. Will you forgive me?"
- "I can totally see how it came across that way. Will you please forgive me?"
- "I am so, so sorry. Truly, I am."

* * *

You have all the tools necessary for establishing and maintaining lovely, life-giving friendships with people who see you, accept you, adore you, and are committed to your growth. And given that you've made it this far in this guide, you're obviously the kind of person who will sacrifice time and energy for things that matter. Which means you'll be a great friend in return.

On behalf of all the best-friends-in-waiting out there: Yay. Yay that someone like you is in the world, and yay that you're every bit as committed to friendship as they wished upon a star you would be.

One More Thing

Can we leave you with a blessing? We'd ask you to close your eyes and really receive these words we want to speak over you, but then you wouldn't be able to read them. Which would be a problem. Receiving them with eyes open will have to do.

Ready?

From our hearts to yours, sister:

May you find your place—a space with ones who feel like home.

May you find your people—ones who are for you and with you and in it for the long haul.

May you find friends who get you and want you—who keep you around and keep you warm when the world turns cold.

May you find friends who let you speak your truth, who know how to disagree in love and how to walk away from an argument but stay close, even when words feel more like stones than bridges.

May you find friends who care enough to tell you the truth you need to hear, whether you want to hear it or not.

May you find friends who value genuine connection, give more than they take, and take conversations out of the shallow end.

May you find friends who make life more fun.

May you find friends who give you grace when you need to come undone.

May you find friends who save you a seat and offer you an invitation and miss you when you can't be there.

May you find friends who point you to the right path when you've gone off-roading and defend you when you aren't around.

May you find loyal friends who stay.

May you find friends who love you—who truly, truly love you—and show you in a way that reminds you that there's a God in heaven who loves you even more.

May you find friends who point you to Jesus, whose light will help you shine brighter, and who will remind you exactly who you are, when you've forgotten the truth of that.

And may you be that kind of friend, too.

Notes

NOTES

Is it just me? Am I the only one who's lonely?
Am I the only one without friends?

9781400226757

If you've ever asked yourself these questions, Amy Weatherly and Jess Johnston, founders of the widely popular "Sister, I Am with You," are raising their hands to say, "Yeah, us too." And they want to encourage, equip, and reassure you that you have what it takes to build the kind of friendships you want.